EVA MARIE

SAINT

BIOGRAPHY

Ground–breaking Life Of A Silver Screen

Hollywood Star That Permanently Altered

The Course Of American Filmmaking

JANE BRYAN

TABLE OF CONTENT

Introduction

Silver screen actress Eva Marie Saint enthralled viewers with her classic roles in some of the most recognizable movies of the mid-20th century. Through exploring the fascinating sections of her life story, we reveal the captivating story that molded a gifted individual who was destined for greatness.

The story of Eva Marie Saint starts in the vibrant metropolis of Newark, New Jersey, where she was born on July 4, 1924. Her birthday had overtones of independence and perseverance that would later inspire her approach to her work.

Saint's early years were filled with a wide range of experiences since he was raised in a household that valued education and culture. She was exposed to the beauty of theater and movies at a young age by her parents, John and Eva Marie, who fostered in her a love of the arts. The foundation for a desire that would grow into an extraordinary career was set by this early encounter.

Eva's ambitions were spurred by the love and support she got from her family, which created a loving atmosphere that allowed her artistic tendencies to thrive. The rich cultural milieu of her family served as a fertile ground for her creative sensibility throughout these formative years, sowing the seeds of her eventual success.

Saint had a natural flair for performing when she was little, often dazzling family and friends with her vibrant energy. She found the transformational power of the stage in her playground, the local community theater. These first attempts at acting were the first signs of an emerging ability.

When Eva Marie Saint enrolled at Bowling Green State University in Ohio, she began her journey from a passionate teenage performer to a promising actor. Here, she devoted herself fully to pursuing her passion for theater and developed her abilities under the watchful eye of seasoned instructors.

Saint used the hallways of the university as a training ground, giving her the theoretical groundwork required for an acting profession. That being said, her fate did not just play out in the classroom. She was able to display her growing skill thanks to the university's active theatrical scene, which brought her recognition that went beyond the school boundaries.

During a summer stock performance, she drew the attention of a talent scout, which was her turning point. This coincidental meeting would turn out to be the impetus that sent her into the glittering realm of Hollywood. Eva Marie Saint welcomed the call of the silver screen with a mixture of joy and dread.

Hollywood in the early 1950s was a place of hopes and dreams, with starlets gracing the pages of glossy magazines and the prospect of fame hanging in the balance. For Eva Marie Saint, leaving Ohio's theatrical embrace and moving to the glamorous glamour of Los Angeles was a turning point in her life.

People in Hollywood were both excited and apprehensive about her coming. Aspiring performers were said to be made or broken in the city of angels, and Saint was standing at the doorway, prepared to carve out a position for herself in the cutthroat world of Tinseltown. She had no idea that her first job as an actress would soon make her name immortalized in the annals of film history.

We will discover the strands of ambition, skill, and destiny that came together to form a star destined for greatness as we delve into this examination of Eva Marie Saint's formative years and her foray into the acting profession. We shall go further into the key positions and turning points that shaped her successful career in the parts that follow, charting the course of an incredible journey that still inspires and enthralls audiences today.

Chapter one

Breakthrough Role

Eva Marie Saint's meteoric rise to fame peaked with her ground-breaking performance in "On the Waterfront" (1954), a picture that cemented her status in Hollywood and permanently altered the course of American filmmaking.

A fortunate piece of cinematic serendipity was the casting of Eva Marie Saint in "On the Waterfront". Saint was spotted at a screen test for the movie by renowned director Elia Kazan. Kazan was struck by her appearance, which was a beautiful fusion of power and fragility. To him, she represented the persona of Edie Doyle.

The role of Edie, a young, idealistic woman trapped between moral quandaries and corruption on the docks, required a performer who could balance resolve and innocence with equal grace. Kazan was persuaded that he had discovered his leading woman by Eva Marie Saint's ethereal beauty and the depth she brought to her screen test.

For Saint, getting ready for the part was an intensive experience. She investigated the social and economic reality of the waterfront location in order to represent Edie Doyle in an honest manner. During his stay there, Saint engaged with the locals and took in the vibe of the docks in Hoboken, New Jersey. Her portrayal was infused with a true sense of the setting because to her systematic approach, which grounded the character in the veracity of the working-class hardships shown in the movie.

There was obvious synergy between Saint and Marlon Brando when they were on film together. Their complex and nuanced relationships gave the drama more depth and took the movie to a level of storytelling mastery that had hardly been seen before. The success of the movie and the start of Saint's extraordinary career were largely due to her dedication to her work and the careful preparation she underwent for the part.

Effect on Profession

In addition to being a critical and financial triumph, "On the Waterfront" thrust Eva Marie Saint into the public eye in Hollywood. Widespread praise for the movie resulted in many Academy Awards, including Best Picture and Best Director for Elia Kazan. Saint's performance as Edie won her the Academy Award for Best Supporting Actress, demonstrating the talent with which she approached the part.

Eva Marie Saint's career was greatly impacted by "On the Waterfront". She went from being a talented up-and-comer to an established actress in the blink of an eye. Saint found herself in great demand as a result of the industry's recognition of her ability to authentically and subtly portray complicated emotions.

The movie's popularity gave Saint access to a wide range of options. Offers to star in high-profile productions began to roll in, and she handled her sudden notoriety with composure and elegance. Producers and directors begged to collaborate with the actress who had made a lasting impression on one of the most renowned movies of the time.

Saint's professional path after "On the Waterfront" proved the lasting influence of a ground-breaking performance. She kept showcasing her flexibility in a variety of genres, including as thrillers and dramas, establishing herself as a leading woman with substance and flair. The movie not only influenced Saint's professional path, but it also created a lasting impression on the film industry, encouraging a new wave of directors and actors.

Looking back, "On the Waterfront" is regarded as a classic of film, and Eva Marie Saint's portrayal continues to be a major factor in the movie's popularity. She established herself as an actor capable of going beyond the limitations of a single part with her ability to negotiate the nuances of the human experience via her character, which struck a chord with both viewers and critics.

When we consider how "On the Waterfront" affected Eva Marie Saint's career, we can see how a breakthrough role may have a profound influence. Not only did the movie launch Saint's remarkable career in Hollywood, but it also established a bar for quality that would guide her future endeavors. We shall go further into the key events and parts that molded Saint's career in the sections that follow, charting her development as an actress whose talent never goes out of style.

Chapter Two

Career Peaks

A thrilling apex was attained by Eva Marie Saint's career, with the classic "North by Northwest" (1959) serving as its high point. In addition to presenting Saint's abilities in a novel way, this Hitchcockian masterwork made a substantial contribution to the changing field of suspenseful filmmaking.

The 1959 film "North by Northwest"

The partnership between the renowned Alfred Hitchcock and Eva Marie Saint was a titanic encounter in the film industry. Hitchcock, who was renowned for his exacting methods in the film industry and his capacity to elicit captivating performances from his performers, saw in Saint a model adept at balancing the delicate line between romance and suspense.

Saint portrayed the mysterious Eve Kendall in "North by Northwest," a woman whose intentions and allegiances are unclear. Hitchcock made a calculated choice in selecting Saint because he knew that she could portray mystery and innocence at the same time. With this performance, Saint was able to show off a new aspect of her acting talent, which differed from Edie Doyle's innocence in "On the Waterfront."

Saint and Hitchcock's working relationship produced a synergy that took the movie to previously unheard-of levels. Saint's subtle depiction of Eve Kendall, along with Hitchcock's methodical directing, produced a figure that went on to become legendary in the annals of film history. With a storyline heavy on espionage, misidentification, and spectacular set pieces, the movie gave Saint the ideal platform to make a lasting impression.

The story was further complicated by the on-screen relationship between Eva Marie Saint and Cary Grant, who portrayed Roger Thornhill. Audiences were kept on the edge of their seats by the intense simmering tension between their characters. The popularity of the movie was greatly influenced by Saint's ability to combine magnetic attraction with a sense of mystery and vulnerability.

The film "North by Northwest" is widely regarded as one of Alfred Hitchcock's best works, and Eva Marie Saint's performance was a major factor in the movie's success. The film's outstanding pace, compelling story, and inventive use of visual effects cemented its reputation as a landmark in the thriller genre.

Eve Kendall, played by Saint, embodies Hitchcock's preference for strong, multifaceted female heroines. Her portrayal gave the movie's examination of identity, trust, and the constant threat more nuance. Cinema enthusiasts will always remember the film's unforgettable final sequences, in which Saint and Grant are in danger atop Mount Rushmore.

Eva Marie Saint's career also changed as a result of "North by Northwest". Although "On the Waterfront" demonstrated her dramatic skills, this Hitchcock project highlighted her adaptability as an actor who could deftly handle the subtleties of suspense and intrigue. Due to the movie's popularity, Saint was able to establish herself as a leading woman who could play a variety of parts and move up the Hollywood star hierarchy.

Additional Significant Film Projects

Eva Marie Saint's career highs went far beyond the Hitchcockian masterpiece, as she was included in several more significant motion pictures that demonstrated her adaptability and persistent brilliance.

One noteworthy undertaking was "Exodus" (1960), in which Saint appeared with Paul Newman. Otto Preminger, the film's director, explored Palestine's complicated post-World War II political environment. Saint was nominated for an Academy Award for her depiction of a nurse caught up in the Israeli battle for independence, demonstrating her ability to play compelling, nuanced characters.

Saint was in a movie with Richard Burton and the illustrious Elizabeth Taylor in "The Sandpiper" (1965). The romantic drama gave Saint a chance to show off her skills in a new genre, set against the gorgeous background of the California coast. Her portrayal of a free-spirited artist added another level to her repertory and added a poignancy to the story.

A notable addition to Saint's resume is "Grand Prix" (1966), a film that pays tribute to Formula One racing. John Frankenheimer, the film's director, starred Saint with a group of foreign actors. She was able to examine the emotional intricacies of relationships under the fast-paced splendor of the racetrack because to her job as the wife of a race car driver.

Every movie project Saint undertook at her career's high points served as a blank canvas on which she could express a wide range of emotions. She never stopped leaving a lasting impression on the silver screen, whether it was in the drama, romance, or thriller genres.

Media Partnerships

The legendary actress Eva Marie Saint made a smooth transition from the silver screen to television, making a lasting impression on the medium. This phase of her career illustrates both her versatility as an actor and her capacity to engage viewers on many media.

A pivotal point in the career of Eva Marie Saint occurred when she moved from the cinematic grandeur of Hollywood to the intimacy of the television screen. Her main platform had been the appeal of cinema, but as entertainment changed in the middle of the 20th century, television began to emerge as a potent narrative medium.

Saint made a deliberate choice of television assignments that let her to go into the character nuance and narrative depth that are associated with her cinema appearances. Viewers could see the breadth of her skill in the comfort of their own living rooms thanks to the little screen, which gave her a fresh canvas and new brushes.

Embracing television was not only a business choice for Saint; it was also an acknowledgment of the changing nature of the entertainment industry. Television provided a unique platform for performers to interact more personally with audiences because of its serialized narrative and direct viewer contact. Saint's shift demonstrated her dedication to the craft of storytelling, regardless of the size of the screen.

A noteworthy television endeavor for Saint was the grand miniseries "How the West Was Won." The series gave Saint a complex character to play as it followed the expansive story of the US government's westward expansion. Her portrayal of Kate Macahan, a matriarch negotiating the hardships of frontier existence, demonstrated her ability to gracefully and tenaciously anchor a story.

Saint was able to explore the intricacies of family dynamics against the background of historical events in the two-season series. Because of the critical praise her performance received, the miniseries became a symbol of television storytelling in the late 1970s.

In the TV film "People Like Us," Saint portrayed a mother who is trying to understand the implications of her son's decisions in life.

Acceptance, love, and understanding were among the issues the movie tackled, and Saint's performance gave the plot more emotional nuance. She received a lot of appreciation for her subtle performance, which confirmed that she could portray the complexities of interpersonal interactions.

In the well-liked television series "Moonlighting," which starred Bruce Willis and Cybill Shepherd, Saint had a noteworthy cameo. Being Maddie's mother gave the program an additional emotional depth and demonstrated Saint's ability to fit in with well-established television genres. Saint's appearance in the episode is still remembered as a high point in the history of the show, demonstrating how popular she is.

Recognition and Awards

Critics and colleagues in the business did not overlook Saint's contributions to television. She received recognition for her work in the medium with nominations and prizes, including one for an Emmy for her performance in "How the West Was Won." This honor further cemented her reputation as a versatile actress who can command attention in any platform by highlighting her impact and smooth crossover to television.

In addition to broadening her skill set, Eva Marie Saint's television endeavors helped to shape the perception of television as a credible and influential medium. Saint's talent to portray people who spoke to the human condition kept drawing viewers in as she made her way into tiny screens and into their homes.

In hindsight, Saint's move to television is evidence of her continued significance in the rapidly changing entertainment industry. Her entry into the field demonstrated her versatility as well as her dedication to delivering complex stories in all of their nuances. Examining the tapestry of her television endeavors, we see an experienced actress handling the changing business conditions with the same elegance and skill that characterized her film career.

Chapter Three

Personal Life

Celebrated for her charm and acting skills on television, Eva Marie Saint has had a colorful personal life influenced by her relationships, family, and her significant influence on Hollywood society. Examining the subtleties of her personal story reveals a complex individual whose life outside of the spotlight is just as fascinating as the roles she portrayed.

A tapestry of love, friendship, and family ties forms the foundation of Eva Marie Saint's private life. Her marriage with producer and director Jeffrey Hayden, which lasted over 60 years until his death in 2016, is evidence of the resilience of partnerships in the volatile entertainment industry.

Theirs was an unlikely Hollywood romance that persevered through the ups and downs of celebrity and the grueling demands of show business. Respected professionals in their domains, Hayden and Saint were cognizant of the difficulties and rewards that come with a life devoted to the arts.

The couple's dedication to one another served as a pillar of stability in a field known for its fleeting nature. Their lengthy marriage served as an example for many, providing a window into a world where love could flourish even in the middle of Hollywood's glitter and splendor.

Being a mother gave Saint's life even another level of satisfaction. In addition to her thriving business, raising their two children, Darrell and Laurette, became a priority. Saint's perseverance and commitment to the principles that grounded her personal life are shown by her ability to juggle the demands of Hollywood with those of her family.

Saint developed enduring contacts outside of her own family among the close-knit group of performers and filmmakers. Her relationships with celebrities like Grace Kelly, her co-star in "Raintree County," and Cary Grant, with whom she co-starred in "North by Northwest," demonstrated the bonds that went beyond the screen. These interactions demonstrated Saint's capacity to build sincere ties in the sometimes cutthroat and ephemeral entertainment sector.

Hollywood Culture Impact

The influence of Eva Marie Saint on Hollywood culture goes much beyond her work in film. Being a pioneer at a time of changing social mores and conventions, Saint was essential in forming Hollywood's cultural milieu.

Saint came to prominence at a period when Hollywood often restricted women's roles to clichéd tropes. Her career, however, disregarded these restrictions. In contrast to the one-dimensional images of women that were common in the 1950s and 1960s, Saint personified depth, strength, and fragility via characters like Eve Kendall in "North by Northwest" and Edie Doyle in "On the Waterfront."

Saint played parts that defied expectations and showed women as complex human beings, which helped to gradually change how the industry saw female characters. Her influence opened doors for actors in later generations who wanted to play parts that went beyond stereotypical gender norms.

She offered Hollywood a special fusion of grace and genuineness. Saint's approach to her profession stressed both elegance and substance, which was important in an age when beauty often outweighed substance. Her graceful manners both on and off film established a benchmark for elegance that went beyond the fads that come and go in Hollywood.

Saint's classic elegance and subtle splendor on the red carpet became a defining characteristic of her identity. Saint's ability to radiate elegance without compromising authenticity in a field where image is carefully manicured helped to spark a cultural movement that emphasized content above appearance.

She handled the shifting realities of the business with elegance as Hollywood changed throughout the years. She adjusted to the changing environment from the heyday of film to the emergence of television and digital media, demonstrating that staying in Hollywood demands not only skill but also a great awareness of current business trends.

Saint's openness to taking on a variety of roles in both television and movies demonstrated a flexibility that appealed to viewers of all ages. By doing this, she established herself as a representation of lasting significance, proving that in a field notorious for being fickle, brilliance and flexibility are everlasting qualities.

Film Industry Contribution

Eva Marie Saint's enduring contributions to the film business are woven into a tapestry that is her legacy in the industry. Saint's legacy endures beyond time, inspiring and resonating with audiences all around the globe with her ground-breaking performances and lasting influence on Hollywood culture.

Input to the Motion Picture Industry

Eva Marie Saint's contributions to the film business are distinguished by her dedication to her art, her adaptability to different roles, and her capacity to bring her talents to every endeavor.

Artistic Versatility: Saint's career shown an amazing breadth across a variety of personalities and genres. She showed that she could play characters with delicacy and sincerity in everything from the brutal reality of "On the Waterfront" to the suspenseful mystery of "North by Northwest" and the emotional depth of "Exodus."

In addition to showcasing her acting abilities, her willingness to play a variety of roles helped to increase the representation of women in movies. During a period when actresses were often restricted to narrowly defined stereotypes due to limited opportunities, Saint's career choices demonstrated a desire to show women as multifaceted, nuanced human beings.

Partnerships with Renowned Directors

Saint has worked with some of the most renowned filmmakers in movie history, as seen by his career. She costarred with Elia Kazan in "On the Waterfront" and Alfred Hitchcock in "North by Northwest," contributing to motion picture classics that shaped their respective periods.

She worked with filmmakers such as Otto Preminger on "Exodus" and John Frankenheimer on "Grand Prix," demonstrating her adaptability to a variety of artistic settings. These collaborations helped the directors Saint worked with leave behind stronger creative legacies in addition to advancing Saint's career.

Sturdiness and Flexibility

Saint's long career spans many decades, which is evidence of her flexibility in the face of the film industry's constant change. She gracefully rode the waves of change, giving performances that endured through the ages, from Hollywood's golden period to the emergence of television and beyond.

In a field known for its transient nature, Saint's versatility and dedication to quality enabled her to stay relevant. She showed that a great creative legacy is not limited to a certain period but rather is built through a commitment to adapt and explore by embracing many media and genres.

Recognition and Awards

Numerous accolades and awards have been given to Eva Marie Saint in recognition of her skill and services to film. These honors highlight her contributions to the film industry overall as well as her particular accomplishments.

Saint received the Academy Award, the highest honor in the film business, for her performance as Edie Doyle in "On the Waterfront." Beyond being a personal victory, this prize was significant because it demonstrated Saint's dedication to her work and her capacity to provide performances that deeply connect with audiences.

After taking home the Oscar for Best Supporting Actress, Saint elevated herself into the upper echelons of Hollywood society. Her acceptance speech was marked by gratitude as well as a feeling of obligation to the performing arts.

Saint received positive reviews after making the switch to television, and her role in the film "People Like Us" got her nominated for an Emmy. Her ability to provide strong performances in a variety of settings was highlighted by this accolade from the television industry.

Saint's nomination for an Emmy further cemented her influence on both large and small screens and established her as a talent who can cross over from cinema to television.

2018 saw the heartfelt presentation of an Honorary Academy Award to Eva Marie Saint in recognition of her ongoing contributions to the motion picture industry. This esteemed award honored her career of accomplishments and recognized the decades-long cultural effect she had in addition to the roles she played.

The honorary Oscar perfectly captured the appreciation of the film industry for Saint's remarkable career and her influence on the direction of American filmmaking. It was a moment that confirmed her enduring impact in the annals of cinema history while simultaneously paying tribute to the past.

The star on the Hollywood Walk of Fame for Eva Marie Saint is another timeless representation of recognition. This star, which was given to her in 1991, is a physical representation of her services to the entertainment sector. The star is permanently etched in the famous sidewalk, symbolizing her influence on Hollywood culture and her position in moviegoers' hearts.

Eva Marie Saint's name is associated with the film industry's titans when it comes to accolades and awards, which is evidence of the enduring influence she has had on the business. Every honor she receives is a testament to both the industry's appreciation of her unique skill and her influence on the development of acting and movies.

She left behind a legacy that continues to this day throughout the history of film. Her achievements to the film business, which include working with renowned filmmakers, showcasing her creative range, and leaving a lasting impression on Hollywood culture, establish her as a pioneer whose influence goes far beyond the silver screen. While accolades and awards are visible indicators of her success, her performances' lasting impact and the lasting impression she has had on the cinema narrative genre are the real testaments to her legacy.

Chapter Four

Involvement in Industry Developments

As Hollywood's heyday came to an end, Eva Marie Saint's subsequent years proved to be a monument to her unwavering love of performing, her flexibility in the face of constant change, and her involvement in the events that molded the film business. This period of her life is characterized by resiliency, reinventing herself, and a persistent dedication to the art that shaped her remarkable professional journey.

In her senior years, Eva Marie Saint shown an unwavering commitment to her art. Saint exceeded expectations in a field that often ignores actresses as they become older, demonstrating that ability has no age restrictions.

Saint was able to get jobs that showed off her depth and variety even though the business has historically tended to give older women less significant roles. Her performances in movies such as "Nothing in Common" (1986), in which she portrayed Tom Hanks' mother, showed that she could bring life and emotional depth to supporting parts.

These performances in later years confirmed Saint's reluctance to conform to age-related prejudices. Her ability to portray a range of emotions, from maternal tenderness to humorous timing, was indicative of her enduring skill and her continued significance in the industry.

Appearances on Television and Guest Roles

One other venue for Saint's pursuits in the latter part of the year was television. Making cameos on well-known programs such as "CSI: Crime Scene Investigation" and "Law & Order: Special Victims Unit" helped her establish a connection with a new audience and showed her adaptability to many genres.

Saint's presence added a seasoned gravity to his later television performances that enhanced the story. Her versatility and continuing appeal to audiences of all ages were highlighted by her ability to fit in seamlessly with the ensemble cast of modern productions.

Throughout her latter years, Saint often turned to theater, which offered her a new platform to display her acting abilities. She liked the intimacy of live performances, from regional to Broadway, and enjoyed connecting with audiences in an environment where every detail is amplified.

Saint's engagement to the acting profession in its purest form was reaffirmed on stage as she was able to explore both current plays and classical pieces. Her theatrical endeavors revealed a performer who, in her senior years, never lost her appetite for the difficulties and excitement that came with taking part in live performances.

Through voice acting and narration, Saint discovered new ways to express herself outside of the public eye. Her unique voice, which was a defining feature of her on-screen persona, worked well for narration in documentaries and animated movies alike.

By doing voice work, Saint was able to use her ability for a variety of projects and connect with audiences in various ways. As the entertainment industry changed in the final years of her career, her voice became a familiar and reassuring feature in a variety of audiovisual products.

In her final years, Eva Marie Saint's persona was not limited to her roles on screen; she also saw and took part in the revolutionary changes that fundamentally altered the cinema and television industries.

As ageism and representation in Hollywood started to become a problem, Eva Marie Saint became a voice for older actors. She defied industry conventions by continuing to get significant parts beyond an actress's prime, and she used her position to advocate for varied and accurate representations of women in media.

Saint's activism served to advance the careers of upcoming actors in addition to helping her get jobs. She promoted the concept that talent should not be limited by age and that tales featuring older people should be conveyed with sincerity and subtlety via interviews and public appearances.

In her later years, Saint took on the role of industry mentor. Her extensive expertise turned into a useful tool for up-and-coming performers, and she actively interacted with prospective actors, giving them advice and encouragement.

Saint gained inspiration and knowledge from her involvement in industry events, panel talks, and one-on-one encounters with young performers. Her openness in sharing her experience—both the setbacks and the victories—helped to maintain a feeling of continuity in a field that often depends on knowledge transfer between generations.

In her senior years, the film industry gave Eva Marie Saint a number of accolades and recognitions in commendation of her lasting influence. In addition to her Honorary Academy Award, she was recognized as a living legend by colleges, industry associations, and film festivals with awards.

When Saint accepted these accolades, it often happened at the same time that she was considering how the business had changed. She offered insights on the shifting dynamics of Hollywood and the value of embracing diversity—not just in terms of age but also in tales and perspectives—whether she was the keynote speaker or the honored guest.

Eva Marie Saint took use of the possibilities given by new media at a time when streaming services and digital platforms ruled the market. She was able to interact with followers directly on social media, share professional tales, and voice her opinions about emerging trends in the business.

Saint showed that he was prepared to change with the times and accommodate the changing ways that people are consuming media by interacting with the digital world. Her use of social media sites like Twitter and Instagram demonstrated her openness to fans and her recognition of the influence of technology on modern entertainment.

To sum up, the last years of Eva Marie Saint's work represent a noteworthy phase in her multigenerational career. Her ongoing acting pursuits, involvement in business advancements, and dedication to activism demonstrated not just her versatility but also her unwavering love for the performing arts. She rose to prominence off-screen and added to a wider discussion about ageism, representation, and the dynamically shifting nature of the entertainment business. Saint's legacy developed as each stage of her career came to a conclusion, making a lasting impression on cinema's past, present, and future.

Chapter Five

Examining the Influence of Eva Marie Saint

Eva Marie Saint's career in Hollywood is a tale of brilliance, tenacity, and enduring influence on narrative technique. We find ourselves enmeshed in the legacy of a real cinematic star as we consider her remarkable career, the periods of her life, and the lasting impression she had on the entertainment business.

The influence of Eva Marie Saint on the motion picture business is not limited by time or genre. Her performances, which were distinguished by an uncommon fusion of power and vulnerability, brought to life characters that had a profound emotional impact on the audience. The grimy docks of "On the Waterfront" to the exciting mystery of "North by Northwest," Saint's versatility in playing a variety of parts demonstrated a level of talent that was unique to her day.

Thinking back on Saint's influence goes beyond the screen. Her determination to let age or social norms limit her changed how women were seen in Hollywood. Saint's breakthrough performances in later years acted as a call to action for the enduring value of talent in a field that is known for writing off women as they become older. Her support of varied and genuine representations as well as her mentoring of up-and-coming talent demonstrated her dedication to promoting equality and longevity in the business.

Having seen the revolutionary changes in Hollywood, Saint participated actively in industry discussions, embraced new media, and established a digital footprint. Her readiness to change with the times and tell stories in new and innovative ways showed a progressive attitude that appeals to both digital natives and traditionalists.

Beyond her singular accomplishments, Saint's influence is pervasive throughout the development of Hollywood culture. Her involvement in industry conversations, her partnerships with renowned filmmakers, and the accolades and prizes she has garnered all help to create a legacy that goes far beyond the confines of the silver screen.

Eva Marie Saint leaves a lasting and diverse impact in the entertainment industry. It is a testament to her talent's timeless quality, the range of her accomplishments, and the deep impact she had on the history of American film.

Her legacy is reflected in the characters she played, all of whom serve as examples of her talent for bringing the written word to life. From the naivety of Eve Kendall to the mystique of Edie Doyle, Saint's characters became icons in the collective memory of movie buffs. Her legacy is an anthology of performances that speak not just as celluloid scenes but also as timeless moments that encapsulate the essence of what it means to be human.

Beyond her successes on film, Saint is known for her campaigning and mentoring. Authentic representation, daring industry standards, and nurturing up-and-coming talent were all essential elements of the legacy she created. Saint's legacy serves as a living link between Hollywood's golden period and the modern world, emphasizing the value of flexibility, tenacity, and a dedication to the elements that make up outstanding narrative.

Eva Marie Saint's achievements in the entertainment business are shown by the accolades she has received, such as her star on the Hollywood Walk of Fame and the Honorary Academy Award. Every honor she receives, whether from the movie business or organizations honoring her efforts, is a concrete reminder of her impact and ongoing presence.

Conclusion

In summary, Eva Marie Saint's biography unfolds the extraordinary journey of a talented and resilient actress, spanning over seven decades. From her early days on Broadway to her iconic roles in films such as "On the Waterfront" and "North by Northwest," Saint's capacity to engage audiences with authenticity and versatility is unmistakable.

Her career witnessed both triumphs and challenges, with Saint navigating Hollywood's ever-changing landscape with grace and determination. The pivotal moment of her Oscar-winning performance in "On the Waterfront" solidified her status as a formidable presence in the film industry. Beyond awards, Saint continued to tackle diverse roles, showcasing her acting range and dedication to her craft.

The biography also delves into the personal facets of Saint's life, adding depth to her narrative. Her enduring marriage to director Jeffrey Hayden and commitment to family underscore the values that anchored her amidst Hollywood's glitz. The book explores the intricacies of her relationships, shedding light on their influence on both her personal and professional journey.

As readers journey through the pages of this biography, they gain insight into the evolution of the entertainment industry through Saint's experiences. Her resilience in the face of evolving norms serves as an inspiration for aspiring actors.

Eva Marie Saint's life, as depicted in this biography, is a rich tapestry woven with talent, tenacity, and timeless performances. Her legacy lives on not only through the characters she portrayed on screen but also through the lasting impact she made on the history of cinema. This biography stands as a tribute to a woman who, with elegance and authenticity, carved a unique path in Hollywood's history.

Printed in Great Britain
by Amazon

46117597R00036